Earning a Full Time Income: Selling Clothing on EBay A Complete Guide

Copyright © 2014 Conceptual Kings.

All are rights reserved. This book or any portion thereof may not be reproduced or used in any manner whatsoever without the express written permission of the publisher except for the use of brief quotations in a book review.

Introduction

EBay is one of the largest online marketplaces in which users can join to start their online selling business. The great thing about using this platform is that anything that has value to you or your clients can be sold for a price. It even offers an auction type pricing mechanism that allows users to bid on an item and get it for a reasonable price.

Business owners have made money on EBay and that is when they follow the rules and learn the different tricks of the trade that enables success.

This Book seeks to explore the different ways individuals can make money selling clothes on the EBay platform.

1. Pre-owned Clothing
   Some persons may be picky when it comes to clothing and some just may not be. A majority of users who come to EBay come there to seek bargains. They may not mind at all looking at pre-owned clothing as it will save lots of money. Therefore a store specialising in this may be an option.

2. Thrift Stores
   If you shop at local thrift stores you may find items that look great at a cheaper cost. Sometimes persons donate great items to these places and you can catch a good deal. This can lead you to upsell the items in EBay for a good price and make a great profit. You can use

these stores to stock your business.

3. Garage Sales
   Garage sales are another great place you can look forward to getting great deals. Many times persons want to get rid of stuff that are still very valuable and they sell it very cheap. This is another great way to get good merchandise to stock your online EBay store.

4. Discounts
   You also have to be very sharp and look out for stores that are selling discounted merchandise. Many times local stores have sales and mark down clothes and sell far below market value. This again is a great way to stock up on your

merchandise to sell in your store.

5. Quality Pictures
Take quality pictures so that your clients can see the merchandise up close and be able to decide fully if they want it. Especially when it comes to clothing it is wise to take a full picture at all angles so the prospective purchaser can see it in detail to know exactly what they are buying.

6. Weight
It is wise to know the weight of the items you are selling. The weight can influence the shipping costs so you will want to know all of these details beforehand so you can give accurate pricing. If this is not known it can open the

possibility of you making a loss on your item.

7. Shipping
   For small clothing items you have the option of shipping in poly bags and not in boxes that will increase the shipping costs. Poly bags will be lightweight and easier to handle in shipping so this can be a cheaper alternative to the purchaser. They will appreciate that you consider them in the shipping aspect of the purchase.

8. Free shipping
   There are many free shipping options that are available through the USPS. You should get familiar with the options and let them be available to your

prospective clients. Some clients shop EBay stores to see which ones offer free shipping, which to them will be a greater bargain. A free shipping logo or insignia on your online store will help to attract more clients to your business.

9. Fast Shipping
Another important thing to note is the availability of fast shipping. It is a good idea to try and ship within the first 24 hours of receiving payment. The buyers feel very secure in the vendor once they aim to complete the transactions as soon as possible. Once you have shipped, it is good to provide a tracking number to the client so

they can track their package and keep themselves updated.

10.   Children's Clothes
If you are into selling children's clothing you can choose to sell the pre-owned clothing of your children as well. Many times children outgrow their clothing and the clothes are still in great condition. This can be a great resource for stocking your business as these clothes can be considered next to new once your children took care of them

11.   Backgrounds
When taking pictures sometimes you have to consider the backgrounds you are taking against. Some backgrounds do not display the item

properly and you would want the best view for your item. Therefore having a neutral place to take pictures will be good to maintain consistency and have an official look.

12.   Sets
Sometimes selling clothing sets can be a better approach to selling in your online store. Also even if you sell the merchandise apart, the fact that the items are linked it can possibly lead to a return customer that will come back to purchase the additional piece they need. Sets create that linkage that some customers need to create and have loyalty to a vendor.

13.   Templates

There are selling templates that are available to setup your online store. What this does is to get a seller up to speed quickly and have your business looking professional and elegant. This will ensure that you can focus on your stock and selling instead of being focused on aesthetics. The templates will have you up and running in no time.

14. Acronyms

Sellers on EBay use acronyms to describe their merchandise in the item description some users can get an idea of what is contained on the item page. These items let the consumer know whether the items are New, New without tags, like new, good condition etc. These acronyms are a quick way for them to identify the condition of the item.

15. Like new items
For items that are not new or in any other condition than new, it is wise to have a great photograph to clearly indicate the condition. You may have used the description to describe what you are selling and sometimes users may interpret conditions differently. Therefore posting a detailed picture removes the ambiguity so it is quite clear what the condition is.

16. Creative Persons
For the creative person who can make clothing, having an EBay store is a great way to market

and sell your clothing. You have the option of even selling made to order items on the marketplace. This is an excellent approach to getting your items out there and creating interest in them.

17. Preparing items to sell
When selling clothes you have to thoroughly inspect the items to make sure they are in good order to be sold. You have to make sure the items you are listing are in a good enough order to be sold and you properly describe it to the purchaser. If the item is in subpar condition it should be clearly stated and pictures displaying condition.

18.   Listing
Before being able to sell you must prepare the listing to be seen. The item description is very important as in many cases this is what the consumer interacts with first. You must be clear and honest in your description about the product and give all details that are necessary. Accurate pictures will complete the description to ensure accuracy of the product.

19.   Your store
The items are not the only thing that will lead the customers to your purchase from you but your store can be a great promotional tool. Your store can drive traffic to gain more shoppers to do business

with you. Populate your site with enough information to make it appealing to users of EBay, the more information provided the more comfortable persons will feel doing business with you. Also after doing a great amount of business you will be awarded a top seller ribbon to assign to your site.

20.   PayPal
Getting a PayPal account is another great way for you to interact with EBay. This allows transactions to be reliable and safer for buyers and sellers. They have enough fraud protection to ensure that a fair deal is done in each transaction. It eliminates the chance of being scammed and allows

instant transfer of money.

21. What's popular
When going into the area of clothing it is wise to know what styles are popular for our target audience. Persons have different tastes and fashion styles so you must know what is popular amongst your targets. Also it is wise to carry accessories and shoes that will go well with the clothing selections.

22. Name Brands
Again depending on your target market they may be looking for name brand clothing which will be attractive to them. It doesn't matter

if they are new or pre-owned they just want to know they are looking at a popular brand of clothing.

23.   NWT
Brand new clothing or New with Tag (NWT) are always a big draw for persons as this will be first hand to them. The fact that they will be getting a deal and nobody has warned them before will attract persons to the item.

24.   Vintage
Vintage items are another top selling group of items on EBay. This will include one of kind fashions that are hard to get or are no longer made. These will be in big demand and you are able to hold out on price because they are rare items. This is

popular among sellers as they can make a lot of money in this area.

25. Sample Sales
This is a great way to access multiple items of clothing at a cheap price. Designers may be releasing their clothing samples early before the season to test the market and you can get in at this time. If you manage to get clothing in this manner you will be getting them at far below the market rate. Therefore you can make a good profit on it when you sell it in your business.

26. Wholesale
This is the traditional way of conducting business in a brick and mortar store and this can be translated into your EBay business as well. You can buy your

goods wholesale from manufacturers and then sell it retail in your business. This traditional way of business works fine and will gain you decent profits as well.

27. Seasonal sales
In the clothing business, some retail suppliers will have seasonal sales and drop their prices. Therefore you can use this time to stock up your business for a later period based on the discounts you will be getting. For example sweaters and warm clothing can sell up to 90% off in the summertime.

28. Discount Stores
Large retail stores in the industry have a way to offload some of their extra stock that may not have sold when it was

originally released. They send the clothes to discount stores that will mark them down to get rid of them even as much as 75%. It is the same great clothes you come to expect from high fashion clothing, making them a great place to stock up for your business.

29. Mailing lists
Mailing lists are a good way to keep up to date with the large suppliers to know when they are having discounts. This will ensure that for every time a discount is coming you will be informed of the possibility of savings. The mailing lists can also let them know when they are getting deliveries so you can stay on top of the merchandising.

30. Your mailing lists
Similar to how the bigger retailers have their mailing lists you can set that up for your clients. This is a good way to keep in touch with your clients and brief them of developments in your business. This is another good way to introduce new items and push more traffic to your EBay store.

31. Estate Sales
Estate sales are another innovative way for you to get items that may still be in good condition. This will simple be items that the estate may want to dispose of as the person is no longer around to use them. You may get lucky and find good stuff in a sale like this.

32.   Flea markets
Great deals can also be found at the flea market as not everything sold here is inferior. Many times persons give their things to be sold here and it is still in good condition. You may get lucky and pick-up a good deal and be able to resell this item into your business.

33.   Predatory tip
Sometimes they are other sellers on EBay that may not be practicing the best operational practices and their store may not be so popular on the site. However they may be selling great merchandise but do not have the know-how to get it properly advertised. You may purchase these items and then upsell them in your store as

maybe you have more traffic than they do.

34. Track your sales
To fully know if you are making money it is wise to track all the revenue and expenses you have in operating the businesses. Once you have all your data you can evaluate the position of the business to know exactly where you are.

35. Research
It is wise to do some research in the clothing area you are going into to find out the demand for the items. This can help you to structure your promotional activities and find your appropriate target market. There is so much to learn and doing some research will bring you up to speed.

36. It is a job
For you to be truly successful in your EBay business, you must take it seriously, that is, as a real job. This will enable you to focus on what needs to be done and ensure that you remain relevant as you will put the appropriate amount of energy and time into making it a success.

37. Mannequin
In the clothing business, sometimes a mannequin is a good idea that helps to display how clothes will fit. Some consumers may be picky and prefer to see detailed fitting information before they purchase. In business you have to attempt to cater for everyone as much as possible.

38. Inventory

Keep your inventory organized so they can easily be found. This will also help you to always keep the correct inventory count so you will not post wrong quantities. This can turn off clients if they order something and then you respond that it is in fact out of stock. Having an organized space will allow you to get to the item quickly and allow faster shipping.

39. Listing Fees
The more items you list it can save you on listing fees. So it makes sense to start a store once you plan to have over 100 items listed at any time. If you are looking to have a few items then it is best to list them individually.

40. Store linking
If you list items individually and still maintain a store you can advertise the store and post links to it. What this can do is to link new users to your store so they can see the other items you sell. It can help to drive more traffic to your site and in turn lead to more sales.

41. Authentic
Be authentic in all that you do. Especially in clothing, sometimes persons sell knockoffs and portray it as being the real thing. You must aim to sell original clothing and if it is in fact not authentic you need to state so in the posting. This must be clear at all times to potential buyers.

42. Rules

Make yourself knowledgeable on EBay rules as they are made to regulate the site and ensure fair trading. You do not want to violate the terms and get into any issues with the site. This will not be good for your store to be flagged as being in violation of the rules as if consumers see that more than likely they will not feel comfortable to do business with you.

43. Measurements

In clothing, there may be some additional measurements that are necessary for consumers to get the accurate details. This again should be posted in the description to be clear to the consumer so they can accurately make their decision. This will reduce the need for

them to email seeking
clarification and can
lead to them making
quicker purchase
decisions.

44. Strategic Pricing
When pricing clothing
you should browse the
competition to see what
they are selling similar
items for. You will not
want to price yourself
out of the industry as
you want your items to
be relevant. Another tip
for selling is to start
the price with ".99" as
it makes it look cheaper
than it really is for
auctions only.

45. Categorize
You can categorize your
store so consumers can
easily find what they
are looking for. Some
sites do not have proper
navigation which can
sometimes turn off
clients as it may take

too long to find items.
The categories should be
as simple as possible to
allow clients to easily
browse to what they
need.

46. Fees
Get familiar with the
eBay and PayPal fees to
ensure that your pricing
is adequate. These
services take percentage
of the sale price and
you must ensure that
what is left is
sufficient to fund your
profits. Before listing
ensures that you read
how the site works and
what the percentages
are.

47. Niche
For some sellers, having
a particular niche may
work for them. This can
help to promote your
store as one of the

authorities in a particular niche. Once you list your items being a leader in that industry can help you to gain traffic.

48.   Promotion
There are many ways to promote your site off eBay. Articles and Social Media are some of the ways that you can drive organic traffic to the store. Once you place adequate promotion in the right areas it can generate interests to your store. One main thing to remember is to always place links with your promotion so users can find the store easily.

49.   Profit Potential
All businesses have the potential to make a profit. Sometimes you may have to feel out the process of buying and

selling before you find what works best for you. The initial profits may be small but once you get into the right operation you will eventually see that the business will get better. It is a learning process that will take time but once you have the correct steps you will see yourself turning profits in no time.

50. Marketing
Always try to link to your store in most of your online communication. Place links at the bottom of your email communication, your Facebook and Twitter page and everywhere you can think of. This can help to generate traffic to your page and do well for your business.